PENNY TOOGOOD

The Kids book of I am's

First edition

This book was professionally typeset on Reedsy.
Find out more at reedsy.com

Contents

Preface

"Don't beat around the bush"
   What bush my kids would reply!
"I'm only pulling your leg"
   No you're not! You're not pulling anything but you seem to be joking!!

Do you ever find that parents talk in riddles! They have all these saying and in their world they are making sense but for you its really not that obvious!

"Turn over a new leaf"
   " Don't cry over spilt milk"
   " She's as cool as a cucumber!"

Sometimes you can work out what they mean and other times you are left thinking your parents have come from another planet! I mean who on earth would say" Bite the Bullet," or why would you tell anyone to " break a leg!" before going on stage and why do expensive items cost an "arm and a leg?" What about your hand, head or rest of your body? Is that not worth much!!

There are times we hear things and we are left feeling puzzled or confused. That was what it was like for people when Jesus walked the earth. He came to tell them incredible things about how much he loved them and this amazing mission on earth to rescue people and bring them back into a special relationship with his Father in heaven. Yet not everyone could understand what he was saying. It's like there was a secret code.

People whose hearts were open and who knew there was something missing on the inside of them had ears that could hear. That meant that when he spoke they not only heard what he said but they understood his words. Then there were people whose ears could hear the sounds and words were clear but they couldn't actually understand what Jesus meant. It's like their hearts were closed and they couldn't receive his message.

Jesus wanted to show people who he was so he used lots of different pictures to describe himself. You probably know a lot of them.

I am the light of the world

I am the bread of life

I am the way, the truth and the life

I am the good shepherd

I am the door

I am the vine

I am the resurrection and the life

Jesus wants us to understand these saying because they tell us about who he is and how he loves us. In this book we want to help you understand in a deeper way what these words really mean so that everyday you can be assured that Jesus is with you, watching over you, taking care of you and leading you into his incredible plans and purposes for you in this world.

Part 1

I am the light of the world

1

Seeing for the first time

"One thing I do know. I was blind but now I see!"

John 9:26

What does a normal day for you look like?

Do you think you could describe it in less than **10** words?

Go on have a go. Let me try and guess? Would it go a bit like this?

'Get up, eat, dress, wash, school, home, eat, wash, undress, sleep'.

My week could be summed up pretty much the same although I'm no longer at school! For most of us our daily routines are pretty similar. Sometimes we might even complain about having to do the same tasks everyday. Tidying up, setting the table, homework, bedtimes. If we focus on the things in life that we don't really enjoy, we often miss all the incredible things around us.

In the summer holidays I love the blue sky days. In our country that doesn't happen everyday so when it does we try and make the most of it! We head off on day trips to the beach and lose ourselves exploring the rock pools for crabs and exciting sea creatures that lie hidden in their underwater worlds.

In the winter my kids long for snow and I love the mornings when they open their curtains to find a white world outside calling out to be explored. They spend hours making snowmen and having snowball fights until their fingers are so numb they can hardly move them!

In the Autumn one of the things we love to do is walk through all the leaves on the ground and hear them crunching beneath our feet. In the spring we love to see the blossom falling from the trees like snowflakes.

Our worlds are full of colour and variety and everyday we get to experience something new. It could be a new outfit we have bought, a new friend we have made or a new puppy that we have bumped into on our way back from school. Life is full of opportunities and each day we embark on new adventures that catch our eye.

I want to take you on a journey to meet a friend of mine.....

*****

For Jacob everyday was the same. There was little variation. His world was not one of colour.

It was blank. It's hard to imagine a world without light. A world that is just dark. He was born blind and so he had become used to it. The things we just take for granted, like going for a walk, were not so simple for him.

Then, one day in an instant everything changed.

Jacob had heard stories about the, 'Teacher'. He had been told about the people who were supposedly now made well. Everyone was talking about Him. The important people said that you couldn't trust him, that he was a liar who was up to no good. But that didn't really make any sense. How could he be up to no good if people were getting better? Even the news he'd heard about the miracles was incredible. Some claimed that the, 'Teacher', had turned water into wine at a wedding. Now, Jacob knew the scriptures and the only things water had ever been changed into was blood, and that was when Yahweh had worked through Moses in Egypt. But this time the water was changed to wine! And what's more this, 'Teacher', was a man who loved to party and he didn't care who he hung out with. The rich, the poor, even the ones everyone hated, (tax collectors!!). He seemed to make time for them all.

Jacob was sitting outside the temple as he did each day, hoping that the people passing by would stop and take pity on him. Maybe they would show him kindness, maybe they would have compassion. Some just muttered and hurried past. Some believed it was his fault that he was blind, that it was God's judgement on him for the wrong things he had done. But he was born blind! How could he have done wrong before he had even entered the world? He didn't really understand it. But he just waited and hoped that God would remember him. Jacob could hear people arguing as they walked past him. "*Is it his fault or did his parents do something wrong? Teacher, why is he blind?*" They were acting like Jacob didn't exist. Did they not realise he was sitting there right in front of them? He might be blind but he could still hear!

Then it happened, a voice cut through all the noise. It was not that it was a loud voice or a high pitched voice but It was calm and caring. It was strong and yet soft at the same time and when He spoke the others stopped.

"It wasn't his fault or his parents", he exclaimed.

Not his fault? Those words pierced Jacob's heart. It was like the pain of a horrible splinter that had been stuck in your finger, had finally being pulled out and suddenly was gone. Just like that!

In the blink of an eye, the years of worrying, of feeling like you weren't good enough, like you deserved to be pushed aside were all over. The 'Teacher', was talking about him and his voice was full of love. Then he sensed him coming towards him and next Jacob felt something being rubbed onto his eyelids. It was cold like clay and now the 'Teacher', was speaking directly to him,

"Now go and wash in the pool of Siloam."

Jacob knew this was good news. Suddenly excitement welled up inside of him. He almost felt like he was going to burst. He made his way to the pool and washed his eyes with anticipation, but he was already seeing in his heart. He was picturing the new life that was in front of him. The faces he would finally meet. The sights that would match the sounds he had heard all his life. He believed the 'Teacher', had healed him. He believed that he could finally see!!

Jacob wasn't disappointed!! As he washed his eyes in the pool, suddenly, a beautiful golden ray shone across the waters. Figures who he had only ever been able to try and picture in his imagination now had shape and form as they moved about him. Colour finally invaded his world and

4

SEEING FOR THE FIRST TIME

he was now able to share and experience life like everyone else. He was no longer on the outside, no longer on the edge, this man Jesus, had changed everything, he had switched on the light.

"Hold on, am I dreaming? Is this really happening?" he asked himself.
Then he heard the others talking.
"Look he's walking by himself."
"He doesn't need help."
"He can see.'"
"Jacob can see!"

Others were arguing that It couldn't really be him. They could not understand what was happening.

"It is me, I tell you. It's true. I'm healed." He exclaimed.

"But how can this be?" They asked.

Some seemed annoyed. How could anyone be angry about this and yet they were.

"Who did this?'' they demanded!

It was the religious leaders. They were the ones who refused to believe the news about Jesus. They could not accept that He was sent by God. So they looked for some other explanation. They even found Jacob's parents and asked them to explain themselves. The parents were afraid to speak up so they just turned the attention back to Jacob, *"Ask him,"* they replied. "He's old enough. He will tell you what's going on"

Jacob didn't have any problem explaining what had happened. He wasn't interested in the arguments or debates about who this Jesus was or where he had come from. To him it was pretty simple. I mean, what other man did anyone know who could open the eyes of the blind, heal the sick and put the lame back on their feet again. This could only be the work of a man of God.

"We know this man is a sinner!" they told Jacob indignantly . Jacob simply replied, *"Whether he is a sinner or not, I do not know. One thing I do know ....I was blind but now I see!"*

It seemed to Jacob that he no longer was the blind one, but in fact it was these so-called, "important men of God" who could no longer see clearly. God was at work.

This man Jesus is the light, God's chosen one, the Messiah,But it would seem that some people would rather live in the dark.

Prayer

Jesus, thank you for being the light of the world. Thank you for being my guidance through tough times, showing me the right way and directing my path to safety. Let your light shine brightly through me, In Jesus name, Amen.

Part 2

I am
the bread
of life

2

Who brought their lunch?

"There is a boy here who has five barley loaves
and two fish, but what are they for so many?"

John 6:9

Packed lunches. It always appears to be the subject of much debate in our house. What makes a good one, what makes an awful one and who in school always has the best. It's certainly a hot topic on which everyone has their own opinion. One day I threatened to stop making anymore packed lunches because a debate broke out once again over the dinner table and everyone found something to complain about.

" You've given me cheese and onion crisps nearly everyday this week."
 " My apple was bruised."
"I only like ham wraps, not ham sandwiches"
 " You didn't slice my tomatoes!!"

All I can say is I asked in future for all complaints to be put in writing and they would be taken into careful consideration. They all knew I was joking and the real answer was;

*" If you're not happy with the packed lunch **I** am making for you I can easily fix that. **You** make it!"*

Packed lunches can be a life saver though. Can you imagine trying to make it through a whole day at school or work without one! Whatever you choose to have in yours whether it's chicken or ham, salad, soup or sandwich, we all understand the importance of being able to have something to eat when we're away from home.

******

Ben nearly forgot to lift his packed lunch. He was running out of the door in his usual hurry when his mum called him back. Bread and Fish. He quickly grabbed it, stuffed it into his bag and raced down the dusty lane to catch up with his friends. They had heard the rumours that the teacher was coming to town and Joshua's father had seen the crowds that morning heading out to the hills.

Everyone flocked to see Him, to hear what he had to say. He was not like the normal teachers they were used to. Their words were often harsh and cold. They made God appear distant and angry, like He was always disappointed with his people. Yet the "Rabbi", as he was known was different. He spoke with compassion and love. His news was worth listening to. It was encouraging. People came away feeling uplifted, they felt like God really cared. He loved his people and He hadn't forgotten about their plight.

As Ben arrived at foot of the hill with his friends he wondered how they would ever manage to hear what the 'Rabbi' had to say. There were literally thousands of people scattered all across the mountainside. They made their way through the crowds, carefully trying to tiptoe between the groups of men, women and children who all sat glued to their spots, hanging onto Jesus' every word.

You would have thought it would have been difficult to hear what He said but the contour of the hills made the shape of a theatre, and as Jesus spoke from the valley below his words drifted effortlessly across the plains. The people sat for hours upon hours, hungry for more, loving to hear these words that brought them comfort and hope for their future. Ben didn't really understand all the words but they filled his heart with love. On that beautiful hillside there was peace and calm. He felt that God was close to Him in this place.

The heat from the sun was beginning to wane as it started to sink back down towards the horizon. Ben suddenly felt his stomach rumble and looked around on the ground for where he had left his lunch. It was not like him to need to be reminded to eat, but he hadn't seen anyone else eating either. Everyone was transfixed by the words the 'Rabbi' spoke.

Next, Ben noticed some of the Rabbis' followers discussing things amongst some of the crowd. He could see people shaking their heads and looking apologetic but he couldn't quite make out what they were saying.Then they approached his group and he heard one of them address those he sat among;

"Did anyone come prepared with food?"

Ben looked behind him thinking they were probably talking to some of the grown ups, but no one replied, there was just silence. Ben felt afraid to speak up. Perhaps the 'Rabbi', himself was hungry. No doubt after spending hours on the mountainside talking, teaching and healing the sick, he would have need of nourishment and rest. Ben grabbed for his bag and quickly pushed through to the men, offering up the little he had, 5 small bread rolls and 2 fish. It would hopefully be enough for the teacher and maybe a little to share.

Andrew the disciple did not just take the bag but rather ushered Ben over with him and led him through the packed mountain and down to the bottom where the 'Rabbi', himself stood.

Ben approached cautiously, feeling somewhat overwhelmed to be brought before such an important man. And yet when his eyes met the 'Rabbi's', he felt his apprehension quickly leave and his heart filled with excitement. Something amazing was about to happen. He didn't quite know what, but he just sensed it in the air.

" What have we here now young Ben? Bread and fish! My favourite!"

How did he know my name, Ben wondered to himself, let alone what my lunch was? In fairness thought it was a staple when it came to your average Israeli meal. With a glint in his eye, Jesus reached out and took the packed lunch that Ben held out in front of him, then he looked up to the sky and began to tell his father how thankful he was;

" *Bread and fish! Awesome Father, you are so good and give us everything we need and more!!*"

He then turned to his disciples, broke the food into pieces and began to give it out. This he continued over and over, the bread broke but it didn't run out. It just kept supplying piece upon piece. Food was passed from the very bottom of the plain to the highest part at the top and everywhere in between. People sat eating, laughing and enjoying this instant picnic. Delivered at speed with ease and attention to every single person. From the youngest to the oldest.

Eating at Ben's house was always a boisterous and noisy affair, often with someone grumbling they didn't get enough or that someone had taken too much. What struck Ben was the calm and order that accompanied the roll out of this incredible spread. 5,000 men plus all the women and children were fed and yet no one complained they had been left out or that there hadn't been enough. Everyone received as much as they wanted and there were even 12 baskets left over!! (I hope they were given to the disciples.)

What could he say? Where could he start? How could he begin to describe what he had just seen. *"Did you eat your lunch?"* Mum always asked him this everyday. He chuckled to himself as he thought about how to reply. *"Did you have enough, I'm sure you're hungry after being out all that time?"*

Although he was full, it was not simply from a filled stomach, something more had happened. He had received a different kind of food. Jesus had fed him in a way that was much deeper than anything food could offer. He had nourished his heart with love. He remembered a story his mother always told him about how Moses had received bread from heaven in the desert when the children of Israel were hungry. Today Ben had eaten a new kind of bread from heaven given by the man who he would later learn actually called himself the **bread of Life.**

Prayer

Lord Jesus, how amazing it is to know that with you, "all things are possible". When I feed on you Jesus, I know that you are providing for

11

me and not just for all that I need but you are so loving I know your heart is to provide so much more, just like you did for Ben and all of the people in today's story. Amen

Part 3

I am
the way,
the truth
and the life

3

Holiday adventures

"Jesus said to him, "I am the way, and the truth,
and the life. No one comes to the Father except through me"

John 14:6

Have you ever followed a sat nav? They are designed to help you find
new places when you are driving in your car. They sit on your dashboard
and show you a map of where you want to go and a kind man or lady's
voice gives you instructions about where to turn and which road to take.

Well that's the theory! As your Mum and Dad will probably tell you the
Sat Nav doesn't always know best. At times they can take you down tiny
country lanes that are not designed for modern cars or you can end up
on a road that has disappeared under water as it can be only be crossed
when the tide goes out!

One summer we had a particularly challenging time with the sat nav as
we were exploring the countryside for a month in our caravan.

Unfortunately you can't programme your sat nav to tell you which roads are big enough to fit the caravan on. One particular day it showed us a route that promised to save us half an hour off our journey. My gut told me don't do it, but after listening to the nagging from the voices in the back of the car, and my kids asking me the dreaded question, "*Are we there yet*", for the thousandth time I decided to convince my husband to give it a go! So we turned down a road that quickly turned into a lane that then became a track and before we knew it we were heading up a big steep hill into the mountains. I could see the panic on my husbands face as he looked behind in his mirror and began to realise that we were probably stuck in the middle of nowhere.

Now I don't know if you have ever seen anyone trying to reverse a caravan through country lanes but it is not for the faint of heart! After about half an hour of moving backwards and forwards, nearly knocking down gates, scraping the caravan and holding up about 10 cars, we finally got it turned and headed back towards the main road. It will come as no surprise that after this I was sacked from the position of navigator and we decided that from that point on we would no longer listen to the sweet suggestions from the lady on the Sat Nav, even if she promised to save us 100 miles off our journey. It was the highway from now on!

Finding the right way in life can be difficult and like us not everyone always makes the best choice or chooses to listen to the right voice....!

****

Joshua had been told to go to bed but he was the kind of child that didn't like to miss out on the action. He would go off into his room, pretend to be asleep, and then sneak out when he knew the coast was clear. He and his parents lived in the corner of the village square which meant there

14

was always plenty of action, so he would climb up onto the roof and find a spot where he could get a birds eye view.

Tonight was no exception. The 'Teacher', was in town and, after the crowds had dispersed and the hustle and bustle of the day had died off, Joshua heard the muffled sound of voices whispering in a distant corner of the square as the sky darkened and night fell.

Suddenly the voices appeared to be coming closer. Joshua couldn't quite make out who it was. A tree was blocking his view, but from what he could tell it was a conversation between two men and it sounded serious. One seemed to be asking lots of questions, his voice was curious, almost desperate, as if he was searching. The other, patiently answered the questions but the responses didn't seem to be what the first man was looking for. Joshua, who was always being told he was too nosey for his own good, decided to crawl out a little further to see if he could peer between the branches and maybe catch a glimpse of who it was, and find out why the man was so exasperated.

"Rabbi, we know that you are a teacher sent from God".

Joshua recognised this voice, he had heard it in the synagogue. Why, it was Nicodemus! He was one of the most important Jewish leaders. Why was he asking questions about God? He was supposed to be the expert! Who was this he was talking to? Joshua stretched out as far as he could but still he couldn't hear properly, so he decided to climb into the top of the tree. The branches began to creak at the weight of his body and for one moment Joshua thought he was going to come crashing down on top of them. The men stopped for a second and glanced up. But they must have thought it was a bird as they quickly returned to their conversation and Joshua managed to regain his balance. Now that he had a proper view Joshua could make out who Nicodemus was talking to. It was Jesus, the 'Teacher', that had caused so much of a stir the week before at a wedding when he had turned water into wine.

"No one can do the miracles you do, unless God is with him." Nicodemus continued.

"You are absolutely right", Jesus replied. *"Take it from me: Unless a person is born from above, it's not possible to see what I'm pointing to—to God's kingdom."*

"How can anyone be born who has already been born and grown up? You can't go back into your mother's womb and be born again. What are you saying with this 'born-from-above' talk", Nicodemus enquired frustrated by Jesus' response.

But Jesus answered, *"I tell you the truth. A person's body is born from his human parents. But a person's spiritual life is born from the Spirit."*

"How can all this be possible?" Nicodemus asked.

He seemed puzzled at Jesus' words. His eyes were longing to believe but he stood as if he carried the weight of the world upon his shoulders. Joshua wondered why he had come to Jesus so late at night?Jesus said, *"You are an important teacher in Israel. But you still don't understand these things? I tell you the truth. I have told you about things here on earth, but you do not believe me. So surely you will not believe me if I tell you about the things of heaven! The only one who has ever gone up to heaven is the One who came down from heaven—the Son of Man."* Nicodemus looked anxious. Why was he whispering? Was he afraid that people would hear what He was talking about? Surely he wasn't afraid to be seen with Jesus.

16

"I am the Light from God that has come into the world." Jesus continued. *" But men did not want light. They wanted darkness because they were doing evil things. Everyone who does evil hates the light. He will not come to the light because it will show all the evil things he has done. But he who follows the true way comes to the light."*

'Follow the true way'. It was like a light had gone on in Joshua's head and all of a sudden he realised what was happening. Nicodemus and the other religious men were always telling the people what way to live and what rules they must obey. Everyone feared them and feared God too because nobody felt like they were getting it right. When you made a mistake the religious leaders were quick to judge you and tell you what was wrong. They said you could only come to God if you obeyed his rules.

But Jesus was talking about another way. A new way. And this new way was not about judging people it was actually about loving them, even when they made a mess in life.

"God did not send his Son into the world to judge the world guilty, but to save the world through him." Jesus explained.

This is amazing Joshua thought to himself. He was always thinking he was not good enough and had almost given up trying his best,because no matter how hard he tried to be perfect it never seemed to work. He ended up disappointing himself and everyone else, even the teachers in the synagogue had told him he would never amount to much.

"I wonder what Nicodemus will say to all of this?

Joshua realised the voices had stopped. He looked down to see Nicodemus walking off into the night. Maybe he too was going to become a follower of Jesus.

17

THE KIDS BOOK OF I AM'S

But from the way he walked, his shoulders slumped and his head bowed down, it gave the impression that he went away with a heavy heart. He was an important man, and many people looked up to him. Would he be prepared to leave behind his position and follow this Jesus who lived a simple life? Could he bare to be criticised or even rejected by others. Did he dare to believe that God could love him even when he made a mess, or did he think he had to try and save himself from his mistakes?

No matter what Nicodemus thought, Joshua knew that something had changed forever for him. He felt a glow inside. It was like a new path had opened up before his eyes, showing him a new way to live. At times he had felt lost in life, wondering what he would ever amount to, feeling God disapproved of him. But the words Jesus had spoken played over in his head. Had he heard him right. He repeated them to himself to try and get them to sink in.

"For God loved the world so much that he gave his only Son. God gave his Son so that whoever believes in him may not be lost, but have eternal life."

"I don't need to feel lost anymore." he told himself. "or afraid of God".

In fact God loves me and Jesus has come to tell me about this love and make a new way for me. He is the true way and life."

Prayer

Lord Jesus thank you that you loved me so much you sent your beloved Son to die on the cross in my place. Thank you that you have gifted true life to all who believe in and call on your name. Thank you that I am no longer lost but safe in you. Amen

Part 4

I am
the good
shepherd

4

The friendliest dog Ever!!

"Suppose one of you has a hundred sheep and loses one of them. Doesn't he leave the ninety-nine in the open country and go after the lost sheep until he finds it? And when he finds it, he joyfully puts it on his shoulders and goes home. Then he calls his friends and neighbours together and says, 'Rejoice with me; I have found my lost sheep"
Luke 15 : 4-6

Our friends have a dog called Lee- Lee. She's a beautiful border collie.

In fact I would probably say the most affectionate and friendliest dog in the world.

The first time I met her she sat at my feet, nudging my hand with her nose each time I stopped stroking her. While I talked with my friend I could see out of the corner of my eye that she was slowly edging closer to me, shuffling her bottom onto the seat I was sitting on and creeping along the sofa until the next thing I knew she was practically sitting on my knee and licking my face! She just loves people and loves to be as close to them as possible!!

The one thing we have noticed when we go out for a walk with Lee- Lee, is the fact that she always tries to keep us all together. Her instinct as a sheep dog is to herd us. She just can't help herself, it's the way God has made her. This became particularly apparent when we started to go jogging together. Jogging with kids and animals is quite a feat. We looked like quite a spectacle if you were coming towards us. Two red faced adults, carrying bags of supplies and coats that had been thrown to the wayside, two kids with dogs and one child with a scooter.

Between toilet stops, falls and people needing a drink, we never seemed to get a good run at it. The one thing that we struggled to do was stay together in a big group, someone always darted ahead, while someone else needed to tie a lace. Poor Lee- Lee just couldn't cope. She would run from the front to the back of us. Barking at our heels. Her eyes were everywhere. Keeping the one ahead from wandering off and hurrying up the one who was getting left behind. When we were out you could tell she was on a mission. No one was going missing on her watch!

*****

Being a sheep dog and looking after sheep is no easy task. Sheep are a rather docile animal and tend to wander off and do there own thing. That's why a shepherd is so important, to take care of them and protect them from harm. Daniel knew all about being a shepherd. It's what his father was training him to become. But like the sheep, Daniel was someone who often went his own way and it always seemed to get him into trouble!!

"*You never listen!*" Daniel's Mum complained, as he came home covered in bruises after climbing trees or rocks or attempting to jump off the boulders. He was the kid who just liked to do his own thing. He loved the freedom of being outdoors, he loved the open space and that is why he loved to be out with his father in the fields.

Unfortunately he hadn't learned the importance of staying focused on the job. At times rather than worrying about the sheep, his father found himself searching for the shepherd in training.

So you can imagine how excited Daniel was when his Mum literally pulled him out of the tree that morning to go with her to listen to, 'some man'. He hated sitting still and more than that he hated having to be quiet and listen.

"What was all the fuss about anyway?" Daniel thought, *"Those religious men don't understand what real life is like. They're not interested in us. Especially not me, I don't remember stuff, I'll never be chosen to serve at the synagogue or asked to follow a rabbi".*

Arriving on the hillside Daniel looked longingly over to the green fields where he knew his Dad would be. The life of a shepherd was not easy. The winters were harsh and cold in the hills, while the summer sun would scorch you. You always needed to be alert for wolves or the occasional bear. Unfortunately there was also the fear of robbers who would come and try and steal from your flock. Then you had to ensure your animals were healthy, getting plenty of food and water and in a pretty dry climate that was a challenging task.

The hardest part for Daniel was making sure that none of the sheep went astray. This was probably the most frustrating too because let's face it - sheep are not exactly the smartest animals. Admittedly a lot of the time that works to your advantage as they follow the one in front of them.

But there is always one that doesn't do what its' supposed to. There's always one that seems to wander off the path, there is always one that goes its' own way.

Well Daniel shouldn't really complain because as his Dad told him, "*They are a lot like you Daniel! There's always one who thinks he knows better than the rest!!*"

"Suppose a man had 100 sheep", His voice drifted through the air and Daniel's ears suddenly pricked up. Sheep? Why is this religious man talking about sheep! They normally spoke about stuff Daniel didn't understand and he would drift into his normal daydreams of fighting off wolves single handedly, "*and one of them has gone astray.*"

The amount of times Daniel had known his Dad to be checking his flock, asking him to make sure they were all there. This man was speaking a language that was familiar to him. "*Does he not leave the ninety-nine on the mountains and go in search of the one that went astray?*"

Now that is not exactly what Daniel could imagine his father doing. His Father would never want to lose a single sheep. He always tried his best to protect each and every one of them. But would his Father actually leave the ninety-nine to go in search of the one? It could be miles away. It could have gone anywhere, or more likely it could be dead. Snatched by the wolf while out of the shepherds view. Would a shepherd really search and search for just one?

"*And when he finds it, he joyfully puts it on his shoulders and goes home. Then he calls his friends and neighbors together and says, 'Rejoice with me; I have found my lost sheep.*"

This one lost sheep the teacher was explaining about was more important than all the others. The one that didn't do what it was supposed to do, mattered more in that moment than all those who had obediently followed.

This seemed upside down to Daniel but in a way which warmed his heart. He had grown tired of constantly feeling not good enough. Not like the others, never feeling like he made the grade. He always seemed to mess things up, he would always be the one who was seen as the trouble maker amongst his friends and most of the time it wasn't actually his fault. But now whether it was or wasn't him, he always seemed to get the blame. Whether it was at home or in the village people tended to think the worst and he had grown to think the worst of himself. That's why he wasn't bothered about hearing from another teacher who would tell him all his faults and why he didn't measure up to God's standard!

"In the same way, I tell you, there will be more joy in heaven over one sinner who repents than over ninety-nine respectable people who do not need to repent."

So this man was telling people a new message.

Suddenly Daniel understood what all the fuss had been about! Everyone had a chance to know God. Not just the people who had it all worked out. It was all people, like him. The ones who went astray. They wouldn't be forgotten or overlooked; they too were important.

Joy in heaven over him? He had never really thought much about heaven. These words seemed to come alive in his heart. To think God would choose him, a mere shepherd's boy and would party in heaven, imagine God being joyful about him! The teacher continued to explain many things to the people but what Daniel heard changed everything that day.

He stopped being disappointed in himself. He stopped believing he was on the outside. The teacher had shown him that he too could come close to God. Now he wanted to find out more about this man. What was his name, where was he from, who had sent him.

He asked his father that night about what he knew. Apparently his name was Jesus, he was the son of Mary and Joseph, from the region of Galilee. It all seemed very normal and yet he taught with authority and there were stories about how he healed the sick and performed many miracles. He had reportedly fed 5,000 people last week.

But the one thing that Daniel heard, that he cherished the most, was the title the teacher had given himself. It assured Daniel that he could actually become a follower of this new rabbi because it would appear they had a lot in common.

He was not only known as 'Rabbi', 'Teacher' or 'Jesus', He called himself "The Good Shepherd."

Prayer

Thank you Jesus that you are, "the good shepherd", and that like Daniel in this story, I don't have to be disappointed in myself because You are not disappointed in me. You have loved me so much that you lead me and guide me every day. You stay close to me in all circumstances and I never need to be afraid because you have promised to protect me from harm just like a shepherd with his sheep. Amen

Part 5

I am
the door

5

It's a deal!

"Then he took a cup, and when he had given
thanks, He gave it to them, saying,"Drink from it,
all of you. This is My blood of the covenant,
which is poured out for many
for the forgiveness of sins"

Matthew 26: 27-28

"*I'll do you a deal!*"

This became a new phrase a few years ago in our house. It was a saying that Sophie had overheard somewhere and she quickly got the gist of it. Basically you say you'll do something for one person and then they'll do something for you in return. It was a win- win situation. She loved it! The unfortunate thing was no one else was loving her deals because there was only ever one real winner. She hadn't quite got the notion that to have both parties on board you need to be offering something that the other-side wanted.

25

"I'll play on your phone and you can play with my Barbies Daddy."

In Sophie's head this was a fair swap. I mean who wouldn't want to play Barbies? But for some reason Daddy just didn't seem to jump at the offer. Sophie's deals were not having the impact she had expected. She kept getting frustrated as people declined her invitations. She even tried to get you to shake her hand before you had had time to consider what she was saying. This was an attempt to hold you to your promise in a way that she saw as legally binding. Sophie as the youngest child had herself been at the wrong end of a number of bad deals growing up. I would often have overheard the persuasive voices of her brother or sister trying to convince her to swap lollipops. What she took as kindness was actually just the mischievous tricks of older siblings who took advantage of the fact she was a slow eater and who swapped their almost finished lollies for one that was only started. Poor child but I think she has more than got her own back.

*****

Kids just love to make a deal. There were two boys I heard about who were always up to it! Let's find out what the latest is......

"I will help you mend the nets today if you come out in the fields with me tomorrow to watch my Dad's sheep."
    "It's a deal!"
    "Let's seal it! "

The two boys picked up sticks and pretended to make a small cut in the palm of each of their hands. Then they grasped each other's hands and shook them in a strong exaggerated handshake.

The deal was made. The covenant was entered into; they had made a promise like the real men did. They had been brought up to know the importance of making an agreement and keeping your word, so they followed the tradition laid out in their culture that was begun by God himself. Blood from the two parties would be mixed between them showing that their lives were now joined together. Such a bond would not be broken!!

Caleb and Solomon ran off towards the seashore where Caleb's father kept his boat. When they arrived they saw a group of people sitting together. It looked like they were eating lunch as they all sat around in a circle. As the boys got closer they watched as the people shared their bread with each other and then passed around a cup of wine. It was not unusual to see people sharing bread but when they shared the wine they all took a small sip and seemed to repeat some words.

Caleb was always the inquisitive one so he snuck up closer to overhear what they were saying. These people were praying, they were talking to Jesus. Caleb knew all about Jesus. He himself had heard him one day when he was teaching in his village and his friend Miriam had been healed of an awful sickness. He knew that Jesus had been crucified by the Jews who could not accept that he had been sent from God. But Caleb had heard the incredible news that Jesus had risen again. He hadn't seen him but he had heard the reports and he knew that people were still following him. But what did all this mean and what was the ceremony that these people were doing out here on the beach?

" *This is the blood of the covenant.* "

Why were they talking about blood as they were drinking wine? It was all a bit strange. The wine was passed between each one and as they drank he heard another saying, "*thank you Jesus for your blood poured out for us for the forgiveness of our sins."*

Solomon caught up with Caleb and the two boys ducked behind an overturned boat and tried to lean in further to hear what was being said. Unfortunately the boat they were lodged behind was full of dead fish and the stench was overpowering! Solomon's nose began to twitch and before he knew it he let out a loud sneeze.

"What on earth was that?" Joanna looked around to where the noise was coming from.
   " Are you ok?" She called out as she got up and walked towards the boat.

Caleb and Solomon stood up, a little embarrassed that their hiding place had been discovered,
   " We're fine, thanks." Solomon replied. He turned to quickly walk away but Caleb was too curious to let it go, *"We couldn't help overhearing your prayers"*, he started. *" You were talking to Jesus, about a covenant and thanking him."*

"That's right," Joanna said, *"the covenant of his blood."*

" Well Solomon and I make covenants too. Not with our blood but we will when we're older, we know that is the sign of a true promise. But why are you drinking wine and saying that it is blood?"

Joanna explained, "I'm sure it might sound strange if you don't understand the words of Jesus. You see our Fathers in the past made covenants but they were always based on both sides having to keep their end of the bargain. You had to keep your part of the promise or the covenant would be broken."
   "But not Jesus. God sent Jesus into the world to be the perfect man. God

knew we weren't capable of keeping our promises so he sent Jesus to pay the price for all our wrong doing and take our punishment when he died on the cross. His blood was poured out so that we can be forgiven today.

You see we take the bread and break it – just like Jesus showed his disciples before he died. He explained to them that his body would be broken. They didn't want to believe that he would die as they didn't properly understand God's plan. His broken body took all the sickness, disease and effects of sin in the world and it was nailed to the cross with him. Because of this today we remember and celebrate that we can receive his healing and life.Then the wine symbolises his blood that had to be shed to make us right with God."

Caleb then remembered his Father picking out the lambs that were taken to the temple. Everyday the priests had been offering animal sacrifices to God to pay for sin. Now it made sense why Jesus had to die. He came to earth like a perfect spotless lamb and died to save us from death and being separated from God. There were so many things that the teacher said that suddenly began to make sense to Caleb. He pondered for a moment as he thought about all that Joanna had said, then he came up with one more question.

"The day I heard Jesus he was talking about vines and branches. Now I know that wine comes from a vine so is it all mysteriously connected?"

Caleb was enjoying searching for all these clues as he began to picture Jesus in a greater light.

"Well, think about a vine. It is strong. It is at the centre & it feeds all the branches. It gives them everything they need." Joanna answered. *"So Jesus gave us a picture to help us understand just where he wants us to be. We're part of the vine, we're a special part. We're the branches. We feed from the vine. There's only one thing we need to do. Can you guess what that is"?*

Solomon who had been listening the whole time but not saying a word suddenly piped up, '*sit still*'.

Well that's just right", Joanna replied. "*A branch has to stay connected to the vine. If it doesn't it won't be fruitful. So it is with us. We are to stay connected to Jesus. To feed on the words he taught us. To speak to him in prayer, to follow the leading of his Holy Spirit and to remember what he did for us on the cross as we celebrate his supper with the bread & wine.*"

"*So that was it! That's why he had called us branches!*" Caleb said. "*It's all starting to make sense.*"

Jesus had shown that he was greater than death. He was the maker of life and he had gone now to heaven. We can follow him and stay connected to him by remembering what he has done. And he has given us these simple pictures to remind us, bread & wine, branches & vines.

"*I am a branch!*" - Caleb told himself, "*and Jesus you are the vine!*"

Prayer

Thank you Jesus that we are connected to you. You are the maker of life and you have even conquered death. We thank you for what you did for us on the cross. We thank you for communion when we remember with the bread and wine your body broken for us and your blood poured out for us so that we can be wholly loved by you today. Free from all our mistakes and mess. Amen

Part 6

I am
the vine

6

Closing doors

"And suddenly there was a great earthquake, so that the foundations of the prison were shaken. And immediately all the doors were opened, and everyone's bonds were unfastened."

Acts 16:26

Are you someone who enjoys taking a ride in a lift or would you rather just be healthy and take the stairs?

Well, I am always a little wary of lifts because of an experience I had with my first child Ben, when he was about 2 years old. We had been staying in a hotel with my brother and sister-in-law and we were waiting to check out in the hotel lobby. Suddenly the hotel was swarming with people. A large bus full of Italian tourists had just arrived and everyone was piling into the rather small lobby all at once. We had been trying to keep my son and his cousin occupied but they were getting a little restless. With all the confusion and noise we were distracted for a few seconds and the next thing we knew our kids were out of sight. Blind panic gripped my sister-in-law and I as we searched frantically around the corner of the lobby and out of the front door to see if we could see them. They were nowhere to be found. We came back to where we had been sitting and suddenly the elevator caught my eye. There standing inside the lift with his finger poised over the button to close the door stood my son.

In an instant an image flashed before my eyes of the doors closing and my son and niece disappearing into the unknown never to be seen again. We raced towards the doors as fast as we could, praying that we would get there in time. My heart nearly stopped beating as the door closed and the children disappeared from sight. Luckily the kids didn't press any more buttons to take the lift from the ground floor, and as we madly pushed the button in the lobby the lift doors opened again and we quickly pulled them out. We all drew a huge sigh of relief, and the best thing was the kids were totally oblivious to the whole situation. For someone who is always telling my kids to close the doors at home, for once I have never been more thankful to see a door opening!

Sometimes we can't wait for doors to close, like after a busy day at school when we get home and close the door, kick off our shoes and put our feet up. Other times we can't wait for doors to open, when we're heading out to our favourite restaurant, or knocking on your best friends door to find out if they can come out to play.

*****

I want to introduce you to David today, he has an interesting story about what happened when a door opened in his world.

"Catch me if you can!!"

The other kids were always shouting that at David and Hannah. You would think that was a pretty normal thing for kids to say but these kids were not playing the usual game of tag. You see Hannah and David's father worked as a jailer. He was in charge of arresting the criminals and locking them up. That made him pretty unpopular as you were never sure who the Romans might want to target next. Samuel, their father just followed his orders and did as he was told but his kids became the butt of the jokes in the village square. Their so-called "friends" would pretend to arrest them and hold them in their grip. Pretending to be their father the cruel jailer. Their father just encouraged them to keep their heads down, he said the other kids would eventually get bored but they never seemed to. Then one day everything changed.

Some men had come into the town from another city. Someone said they were Jews and their names were Paul and Silas. They were meeting with the men and women in town, praying and talking to them about the man they called Jesus. Jesus had been killed by the Jews but these men were claiming He had risen from the dead and were encouraging people to follow His teaching. Some of the people did not like what Paul and Silas were doing and stirred up the crowd against them, saying they were talking about things that went against the customs of Rome. The magistrate who was in charge of the town had them seized and threw them into jail. He ordered Samuel the jailer to put them into the inner prison and fasten their feet in the stocks, (chains that were attached to the ground).

Paul and Silas however did not appear to be afraid or concerned about the predicament they found themselves in. At around midnight while they were singing and praying there was a sudden earthquake. It was so strong that the very foundations of the jail were shaken. Immediately all the doors in the prison were opened and the prisoner's chains were undone.

33

Samuel the jailer awoke, and when he saw what had happened and how the prison doors were opened he was terrified. He grabbed for his sword and went to kill himself, believing that all the prisoners had escaped. Paul cried out to him, "*Stop! Look, we are still here. Do not harm yourself!*"

Samuel could barely believe his eyes. There sat Paul and Silas, waiting peacefully and looking intently at Samuel. Suddenly Samuel knew these were no ordinary men. He realised now why people wanted to hear what they had to say. He fell at their feet, trembling. Then he brought them out of the prison and asked them, "*what must I do to be saved?*"

They said, "*Believe in the Lord Jesus and you will be saved, you and your household.*"

Paul and Silas went on to explain about Jesus' love for all people, and how he had given up his life at the cross to pay the penalty for all our sin. They told him that now anyone can receive His forgiveness. Samuel took them out and washed their wounds, next he rushed out to find David and Hannah, he said to them, "Quickly bring your mother, there's some people I want you all to meet". As soon as they all arrived Samuel explained the incredible events that had just taken place. The news about Jesus is real. These men have shown me the true way to God. Jesus is the door, we enter into God's life through him. Samuel was baptised right there and then along with his family. Then Samuel took them to his house and they prepared a feast to celebrate.

Hannah and David realised that they now had an amazing story to tell. They couldn't wait to share this incredible news. And even if the other kids did laugh or poke fun at them what did it matter anymore. Their lives had been touched by God himself. Their family would never be the same again.

Part 7

I am the resurrection and the life

7

Wonder Woman!

"Jesus said to her, "I am the resurrection and the life"

John 11:25

There are times as a Mum when you realise your kids think you are actually Wonder Woman! No matter what the task might be, they think you are fully equipped to handle every crisis that might occur during any given day. There was one particular day in the summer however where I found even my supposed Mum super powers were not working!

"Mum come quick, there's a bird stuck in the tree, you have to help it!"

My middle daughter Hope was completely distressed as she had gone out to play in the garden only to find there was a bird stuck at the top of the tree frantically flapping one of its wings.

"Mum, you have to get it down!!"

Hope's voice was getting more upset, as I stood bewildered wondering what on earth I was supposed to do. The bird was too far up the tree to climb up to it and I didn't even know if it was stuck. I looked at my watch, we were supposed to be at an appointment. I told myself the bird has probably just hurt its wing a little, and maybe by the time we came back it would have been able to rest and have hopefully had the strength to fly away. This sounded convincing and I managed to calm Hope down. We prayed for the bird and I promised that if it was still there when we returned we would phone for Daddy. I was adopting the same mentality as my kids. Surely Daddy super powers will be able to fix this mess!

You have probably guessed that when we got back the bird was still stuck and by this stage not only was the bird frantic but Hope was too! It was time to call on the back up plan!

Daddy arrived home about half an hour later. When Daddy finally walked through the door Hope was sobbing uncontrollably, it was literally the end of the world. Her heart was breaking for this bird and her parents weren't doing anything about it! How could they be so cruel!

I was hoping that Daddy had something up his sleeve as things were not looking pretty! I offered ladders and suggested that my son could go on his Dad's shoulders- which would have been quite a sight as he is 17 and nearly 6 foot tall. But thankfully my husband saw a different way around it. He went and got a saw!

"What on earth is he thinking!"

Poor Hope at this point thought he was just going to saw the bird in half. Slowly Daddy began to cut at a huge branch in the centre of the tree, The branch began to wobble and the bird flapped frantically. Then all of a sudden the branch fell down to the ground. We ran over to see the bird still stuck, we then realised what had happened. It's claw had cotton wrapped around it which had in turn got tangled to the branch. We quickly got scissors and were able to finally cut the bird free.

We could hardly believe it as we watched the bird soar off into the sky. Daddy super powers had worked. Hope could breathe again and so could the rest of us.

There are times when we face problems that we just don't know how to fix. We've tried everything we know to do but nothing seems to have worked. We have prayed and asked God for help but sometimes we even start to believe that God has gone silent. This is what happened to one of Ruth's friends....but she learnt that it's never too late for a miracle!

*****

It's so sad," Ruth's Mum told her. Martha just can't believe he's gone. She knew he was ill but she didn't think this was the end. He never even said goodbye.

I didn't really know what to say. I wasn't used to seeing adults upset as they were always the ones that held it together. They were the ones who were always there for you, to comfort you, and always knew just what to say. Now for the first time ever Ruth found her Mum looking lost, unable to come up with the right words or find the right answers. Martha's brother had died four days earlier. He had suddenly fallen ill but she had not been too concerned. She had sent word to the 'Teacher'. He had healed many people and he loved his dear friend. They knew they could count on him to come and save them in their hour of need. But it just didn't seem to make sense. The news had reached Jesus yet he had stayed where he was. He didn't rush back to save the day as they had all expected. He waited there, and now they had finally heard news that he was on his way, but it was no use. It was too late now! Lazarus was 4 days in grave.

Ruth's mother finished wrapping up the bread she had made and told her to go and collect some fresh herbs to bring with them. The least she could offer her was a simple meal and a hand of friendship at this difficult time. They walked quietly down the road. Their hearts were heavy. What words can you say that will help someone who has lost so much.

"*Deborah,*" the familiar voice cut through the silence and to their surprise they saw Martha running towards them. What on earth was going on? What else could have happened now? Surely there could not have been another tragedy and yet the fact that Martha was running proved that it was urgent news.

"*You won't believe it!*" she cried, "*Quickly come and see for yourselves!*"

As they got closer they could see tears running down her cheeks but her voice was filled with excitement and joy. None of this was making sense. Tears they expected but not running and shouting.... next she was laughing

"*I can barely believe it myself. You have to come quickly and see it with your own eyes!*

Martha grabbed her friend's arm and they ran together back down the lane towards their home. It was strange to see your Mum run, Ruth thought. This must mean something very important has happened if the grown ups, who are always telling us off for running, are doing it themselves!

When we arrived at the house there was a large crowd of people who had all gathered around to see and there in the middle of them all sat the 'Teacher', talking and laughing. *"What was all the fuss about? Why had Martha been running and laughing at such a difficult time."* Ruth's mind was spinning as she tried to make sense of it all. She didn't notice him at first because he had his back to her and then suddenly he stood and turned around to greet them.

"Ruth, Deborah thanks so much for coming! It's great to be back!"

Ruth almost thought she was going to faint on the spot then she pinched herself to check that she wasn't dreaming. There before her, looking her right in the eye was Lazarus. She couldn't take it in. Only a few days ago she had gathered in the same house to comfort Mary and Martha and now everyone was celebrating his life.

Martha began to explain, *"He had told me this would not end in death but I couldn't see it before. My faith had wavered when he had breathed his last breath. I thought it was all over. I didn't believe even Jesus could help him. He was gone, his life had left him. But I should have known that Jesus had a plan. I have seen him deliver others I should have known he would not fail me. As soon as he reached me he told me, "Your brother will rise again." I thought He was talking about the last days when we will finally be in heaven, but Deborah it's a miracle! Heaven has touched earth. Jesus has power over death itself!"*

Ruth could not dispute that it truly was a miracle. There was Lazarus sitting among them, talking, eating and making jokes. He was as real as anyone could be. Ruth had never seen anything like this. Such a turn around – from death to life, despair had turned to hope. The tears were no longer of sadness but ones of joy!

She had heard them all describe Jesus in many ways and there were many names that Jesus used to explain to them who he was. She had heard him say, *"I am the good shepherd"*, *"I am the bread of life"*, but now she knew him by a new name and if she hadn't seen it with her eyes she wouldn't have believed it to be true. He is ...."**the resurrection and the life"**....

Prayer

Thank you, Jesus, for your unconditional love and for your amazing gift of eternal life! We praise your great name today and every day, as our redeemer, way maker, promise keeper, light in the darkness and our Friend who is next to us through it all! Keep us rooted in your word and guide us through our journey in this life. In Jesus name, Amen.

About the Author

Penny has been involved in ministry for over 25 years. She currently lives in Belfast where she is married with 3 great kids. With her husband she founded Exchange Church Belfast, a church family that is committed to seeing the world transformed by the grace of God. She is a certified Executive Coach and facilitator working with some of the world's biggest brands providing leadership and management development programmes. A gifted speaker and leader, Penny uses her experience as a pastor, wife & mum to connect people to the truth of God's love and grace.

Printed in Great Britain
by Amazon

33127593R00036